PRIVATE COLLECTION

Poems

and Writer's Guide

Rennie McQuilkin

Antrim House

Simsbury, Connecticut

Copyright © 2005, 2006 by Rennie McQuilkin

All rights reserved

Library of Congress Control Number: 2005906960

ISBN-10: 0-9770633-1-3

ISBN-13: 978-0-9770633-1-4

Printed in the United States of America

by Van Volumes, Ltd.

Second edition, revised and expanded, 2006

Cover photographs

front: prehistoric pictograph from Canyonlands, Utah (by author)

back: frieze panel, Cathedral of St. Lazare, Autun, France (unknown)

Antrim House
www.antrimhousebooks.com
860.217.0023

For my son, Robin

in whom the arts collaborate

ACKNOWLEDGEMENTS

Grants from the National Endowment for the Arts and the Connecticut Commission on the Arts have been invaluable. Thanks to those sponsors of the arts and to all who have offered advice, in particular my son Robin, my wife Sarah, Edwina Trentham, Norah Pollard, and the members of my writing groups. Thanks also to the editors of these magazines, journals, and anthologies that published poems contained herein, often in earlier versions:

The American Scholar: "After Waterloo, What"
The Atlantic Monthly: "Sister Marie Angelica Plays Badminton," "The Reverend Robert Walker Skates"
The Autumn House Anthology of Contemporary American Poetry: "Sister Marie Angelica Plays Badminton"
Chelsea: "Henri Raymond Marie de Toulouse-Lautrec-Montfa"
Cincinnati Poetry Review: "Diorama"
The Connecticut Review: "The Rector's Wife"
Contemporary New England Poetry, A Sampler: "In Wyeth," "The Reverend Robert Walker Skates," "Sister Marie Angelica Plays Badminton"
The Hudson Review: "The Lighters"
The Kansas Quarterly: "On Viewing the Daguerreotype 'Plaisir d'Hiver'"
The Literary Review: "Desert" (as "Horseshoe Canyon"), "Invitation"
The Malahat Review: "Arrangements in Blue & Gold," "Slow Dance, Villejean"
Margie, The American Journal of Poetry: "On Assignment in Uganda"
New England Review: "Pendergast's Garage"
The North American Review: "War News"
Poem: "In Wyeth"
Poet & Critic: "Merry Go Round at the Wadsworth Atheneum" (as "A Real Scene in the Atheneum")
Poetry: "Bruegel's Players," "Eviction," "Ladders to Glory"
Poetry Daily (on-line): "Bruegel's Players"
Poetry Northwest: "Baptism"
Poetry Now: "Baroque Time Piece" (as "Time Was")
Prairie Schooner: "Last Minute"
The Recorder: "St. Gregory of the Golden Mouth"
The Southern Poetry Review: "First Snow in the Garden of the Geishas," "Moving Mother"
The Texas Review: "An Astonishment and an Hissing," "A Pair of Hoppers"
Verse Daily (on-line): "The Rector's Wife," "Sappho in Concert"
Voices in the Gallery: "In the Garden" (as "Noon at the Gallery")
Yankee: "Advent Calendar"

"An Astonishment and an Hissing" won the Ruth Fox Award of the New England Poetry Club and was part of a collection awarded the Texas Review Chapbook Prize.

Certain poems in this volume appeared earlier in the following books: *We All Fall Down, Counting to Christmas, Learning the Angels, Passage, Getting Religion, First & Last.*

PRIVATE COLLECTION

For Chris

hoping you will enjoy these ekphrastic efforts —

Denise
Feb. 9, 2013

ALSO BY RENNIE McQUILKIN

An Astonishment and an Hissing
(Texas Review Chapbook Award)
North Northeast
We All Fall Down
(Swallow's Tale Poetry Prize)
Counting to Christmas
Learning the Angels
Passage
Getting Religion
First & Last

PRIVATE COLLECTION

FORWARD

MAKINGS

Diorama 13
In Wyeth 14
On Viewing the Daguerreotype "Plaisir d'Hiver" 15

FRAMED

The Reverend Robert Walker Skates 19
Sister Marie Angelica Plays Badminton 21
Last Minute 23
In the Garden 24
The Love Song of Brother Bernard 25
Two Ladies Waltzing 26
Slow Dance, Villejean 27
Baptism 28
First Snow in the Garden of the Geishas 30
Serving Girl with Gallants 32
Five Ways of Looking at a Lightning Rod 33
Eviction 35
On Assignment in Uganda 37
St. Gregory of the Golden Mouth 38
The Rector's Wife 40
Pendergast's Garage 41
A Pair of Hoppers 42
Bruegel's Players 44
Dancing at the Gallows 45
Connemara 46

UNFRAMED

War News 49
Moving Mother 51
The Lighters 52

PRIVATE COLLECTION

The Cane	53
Endangered	54
Henri Raymond Marie de Toulouse-Lautrec-Montfa	55
Arrangements in Blue & Gold	57
Self-Portrait at 14	60
Baroque Time Piece	61
Whittle	62
Kachina Carver	64
Solstice	65
Desert	66
Ghost Ranch Amphitheater	68
Climbing the Tower	69
Sappho in Concert	71
After Waterloo, What	72
Under the Sun	74
An Astonishment and an Hissing	76
Retrospective	78
Advent Calendar	80
Getaway	81
The Cry	82
Merry Go Round at the Wadsworth Atheneum	83
Ten	84
Invitation	85
Discovery	86
Work in Progress	87
Ladders to Glory	88

WRITER'S GUIDE

Ekphrasis	91
The Art of It	92
Notes	94

ABOUT THE AUTHOR	120

DEAR READER

Welcome to what I hope will be an exciting reading and writing experience. The poems in this book, which I have written over the course of forty years, are based on works of art (from crayon drawings to Bruegels) and suggest, I hope, that such poetry can be personal, impressionistic, and not entirely humorless. The poems are meant to be a starting point for your own writing; hence the Reader's Guide at the end. In addition to suggesting writing and discussion topics, the guide gives detailed information on using the internet as a museum and library.

MAKINGS

DIORAMA

Now you see
the diamondback's spade of a head
rear so pointedly
the frog it has in mind

poses as a lump of clay
full of hope
the snake won't know it. And now
you don't

see more than bright glass eyes,
a stretch of hide
on cotton, cork and wire.

Have faith. If those two saplings
and a stone
seem unreal, they have you fooled

until halfway down a limb
or in the midst of lichen
they begin to be pure

fabrication. Come join me here
at the seam between
the one world and the other.

IN WYETH

In Wyeth we never see
so see the more
the thunderheads
an old hound points as if
they are fair game

and do not see
so see too vividly
in pickaxe and shovel
red with clay
at rest against a rotting stump
the old dog's death.

In Wyeth we are not shown
the way a girl who shores herself
on arms like bone
has hauled herself from house
to barn, from barn to field.
We know.

The art is to suggest, not say,
until we see
not precisely the old man's dory
scrubbed and caulked,
its bow line neatly coiled
in the bone-dry loft of a barn,

and not precisely loss, or all
that makes loss
gain, but something like
all three.

ON VIEWING THE DAGUERREOTYPE
"PLAISIR D'HIVER"

May my words display some sense of style
like the sports in this daguerreotype:

what handsome homburgs and bowlers
and oh those waxed or walrus mustachios.

May my words take place on lines as set
as the sturdy runners of the sled

these gents in their brown study sit
upon—hickory runners placed well apart,

a rhyming brace of them curled like prows
baroque enough to make a Viking proud.

And may my words kick up their heels, let
loose their vehicle and send it
down such a precipice as will not end
until it reaches Hellein or Grieskirchen.

FRAMED

THE REVEREND ROBERT WALKER SKATES

on Duddingston Loch at sunset
in black—black top hat and frock coat,
britches, garters, stockings, skating shoes
black. Except for pink laces
and the flush on his face, slightly deeper
at the ears,
he is black as this morning's sermon.

Oh yes, his scarf is white. And if I say the ice
is black, I mean it's not, is in fact
a window for fish.

The Reverend has turned his back on the sky
between the hills, which is the color of his ears.

His right leg is raised, extends behind him
like the long tail feathers of some exotic bird.
He is leaning into the wind,
leading with the sharpened blade of his nose,
arms wrapped one inside the other.

Or so Sir Henry Raeburn, R.A., did him
in oils, c. 1794.

Those fine cross-hatchings on the Loch
are not from all the Reverend's parishioners
celebrating after service, skating up a storm,
for the hills and the sky seem no less
skated upon.
It's Time. As surely as ice, oils crack.

Nor is the clerical top hat what it was.

You'll find the ghost of its earlier brim,
painted out imperfectly, is aimed low
as if a moment ago the vicar was searching
for a flashy trout.

He has, it appears, raised his sights
to the deepening blue of night, or something
more distant. He dedicates a miracle
to it, no major miracle, mind you, but still

he makes his turn (notice the sliver of ice
kicked up by the heel of his skate),
has all but completed the figure 6
he means to raise
to an 8.

SISTER MARIE ANGELICA PLAYS BADMINTON

with Sister Marie Modeste most afternoons.
Today, because of lengthy vespers, they are late.
A pale moon has already risen and early bats
are darting like black shuttlecocks.

Except for the whisper of wings
and the Sisters' hushed encouragement,
the only sounds are the plinking of rackets
and a monotone of mourning doves.

On all sides of the court
the sculpted yew in cubes and columns
might pass for black so deeply green it grows.
And now it moves closer,

Marie Angelica would say,
who has been known to have visions.
Though she moves as aptly as the bats,
doesn't miss a shot,

when she fades for a long one
from Marie Modeste, sways on her toes, arches
her back, raises one arm
and the other to keep her difficult balance,

she is lost, a long-legged girl again
in mare's tail, mullein, milkweed,
leaning on the sudden sky as if it can sustain her
like a hand in the small of her back. It does.

Her nerve ends quick as a shiver of poplar,

arms like branches in a wind,
she feels a cry begin
to rise, to force the self before it

and burst, all colors one. That white.
It vaults straight up, a feathered cry
that hovers in the heart of heaven, hovers,
and plummets to the gut

of the racket she sights it in,
the perfect bird, the shuttlecock
Marie Angelica keeps in play, will not let fall
despite the darkness gathering.

LAST MINUTE

Look again. There are crows
slightly darker than the sky
circling that cliff
and more below in the winterkill
around the slough.
They can barely wait.

Center left, a two-horse sleigh
on the edge of the cliff rounds a bend
too quickly. The couple within
is caught by a shaft of sun
through a rift in the sky. In no time
the dark will close on them.

But all that
will have to wait. The scene
is still on its easel, set for the painter
who enters now, biting into a windfall
Mac, his mood much improved.
He adds a dash of red,

small banner—
the lady's scarf expressing the turn
she leans into, insisting
on tea at four, a fire, festivity.
He wishes her well
against the clenching sky, the crows.

IN THE GARDEN

Distilled by Courbet, he lounges on
rock, blunt boot in the foreground
matching dark fieldstone beyond.

His baguette, jug of ordinaire
and hand poised to cut into cheddar
repeat the permanence of granite.

The stone breaker's afternoon labor
of splitting boulders
is beside the point. Time's no more

than that dark coil of cloud in a far
corner of the sky. In this preserve
of noonday amber,

this garden of stone, he'll forever be
about to break bread and cheese,
as timeless as any urned Grecian—

I will have it be so, keep my mind
off that cloud wound tight, its time
come round to strike.

THE LOVE SONG OF BROTHER BERNARD

So much for my homily. It ricochets off Eve,
recumbent, leaning on an elbow
in her allotment on a frieze

among such cautionary demons, grape vines
and constrictors. Has she no shame? As if to scratch
she reaches behind for another Winesap.

Yes, she smiles, *yes, yes,* her head inclined to
a serpentine braid in the ivy.
We can see from the arch of one lush eyebrow

she's not to be trusted. Shame
on me for so enjoying how her hair flows
down one shoulder and over the offending arm

as if it knows no better
and how unrepentant her risen pips.
Whatever has sliced off her hand at the wrist is

right, of course, and I'm wrong to look. But
how perfect the curve
of her throat.

And how deeply in the dark of it
she hums. *After all,* her song would seem
to say, *after all.*

TWO LADIES WALTZING

We are the dancers you placed upon
this midnight promontory
to waltz, moon-washed, to the bang, lap and
whisper of surf, the swish and snap
of taffeta. Small wonder our careful hair came

undone and our dance took
a turn you deplored. Are we more immoral
than the shudder of gold
you lavish on the muscling sea? It does no good
to double the ply of our gowns

and slow the dance, arrange our hair in buns.
Revised, our thighs are all
the more Grecian
for the cling of their apparel.
What's taffeta taut with wind but celebration

of taffeta's dismantling!
Don't scowl so, mister. You made me
close my eyes, nestle my chin on her shoulder,
brush my lips across the tender
of a hand—hers, mine, no matter—

and made our free
hands reach for the breakers
not for balance but sheerest vertigo,
fingers tracing fingers so utterly they shiver
like the brush you would cancel us with and can't.

SLOW DANCE, VILLEJEAN

It's fall in the photo, late fall in fact, judging
by the shriveled leaves on this cul de sac's
deserted hardpan littered with debris—
trampled cartons, tin and sheetrock.

The roadside trees, bare now, are overgrown
with vines. Nailed to the trees, a few boards
dangle, out of kilter,
the last of childhood's rungs.

Center right is a Citröen with a hint of fins,
circa 1957, and leaning against it
a battered Mobylette.
On the horizon a factory blocks the sky

but what a camera's depth of field brings in
is forgotten behind the closed eyes
of the couple in the foreground.
She is fat-shouldered, short, stout-necked,

he not much taller, chin receding,
face discolored jaggedly from neck to temple.
Her hand, loose on his rough wool sweater
over the heart,

is pressed by his. He has his other hand
around her waist, and each has one foot
forward, one back. Their down-turned brows
are touching. He hums their song.

BAPTISM

Things keep going on the way they do
except one day in the middle of nothing
they don't.

I remember how hot it was—not a creak
from the windmill
and the Fords our folks had come in
steamed.

We stood around.
Our pockets were no place for hands,
they said, and wouldn't let us in the dark
of the barn or anywhere God wouldn't be
because the preacher was in the yard
to baptize whoever he could
in Tatums' water tank.

Six lined up.
I envied them the cool of their gowns
and the year or so they had on me
but not the way he dragged them under
and kept them there so long they bucked
like bullheads.

Mostly, I went along with the hymnbook
someone pushed at me—
until he got to Ellen McGee,
held her under and didn't stop,
thinking maybe anything that pretty
was bound for goings on.

I was ready for something like the cat
I had tried to drown and failed
when up she came as sweet...
and stood for a spell at the edge
of the tank, at home in the sky.

And her gown, wet through, was true to her
and her face was where the sun had been.

FIRST SNOW IN THE GARDEN
OF THE GEISHAS

Slowly, each flake discrete, a calligraph,
the snow descends on Kyoto.
The sky is a scroll,
its characters spelling the many names
of Buddha.

In this garden of the geishas, the snow
on japonica, laurel and stone
is elaborated
by the day's last sun, like the youngest geisha
adorned for song, for dance

and pleasures more expensive.
Her face, glazed white,
is deftly painted, kimono tied like a flower,
outlining her nape in red,
revealing the slightest hint of down.

In half an hour the paper lanterns will glow,
the plump-breasted plover on each
an invitation
to the narrow lane of Pontocho.
Half an hour and the shamisen will sound,

the feast begin. Now, she walks the garden,
its pattern blurred by the bright disguise
of snow. Beneath a pretty toy bridge
glide pinioned ducks like polished
courtesans in jade and coral and ivory.

As if to bow, she bends down
to roll a seed of snow
until it is fruit, white fruit.
It grows, unveils the grounds of the garden
where only a year ago she was a novice,

drank saki from the triple cup of love,
wore on her feet the bells
to which her hair, unbound at night,
fell softly as the lavender sleeves
of her kimono.

The dark descends,
the snow fruit glows, and above it
a full-faced moon, glazed white,
leaves the world behind. Far off,
a temple bell. And the shamisen sounds.

SERVING GIRL WITH GALLANTS

First the checkered black and amber tile is applied
on the canvas, then leaded glass, stage right,
is made to admit enough of Delft's astonishing light
to gild the room. Soon it's time

for the tavern's newest treasure,
a slender young woman in maroon-red skirt,
tight-waisted purple tunic and linen-wimpled curls,
demure as the Virgin over the mantle. Half turned,

her small feet prim on a tile, precariously
she lifts her goblet and through its prism sees
those slapdash gallants at table, brushed in swiftly,
to whom she is to sing. The first taps his knee,

the other like a cricket rubs a pair of meerschaums,
winking. Judging by that red-plumed broadbrim
and orange, white-tasseled sash, they come from
the greater world of the provincial map behind them.

That the game is all, its players the usual
pawns, is lost on them, but we see from our remove
a pentimento of chessboard floor shine through
one dandy's handsome pair of oxblood boots.

Upstage, the old serving woman, eyes averted,
who brings a brazier of coals to warm the worldly
assumes her part is to be used. But the girl—
she holds up her goblet by its base uncertainly

as if to shed light on a dark passage. Her Rhenish,
kindling in a shaft of sunlight, trembles.

FIVE WAYS OF LOOKING AT
A LIGHTNING ROD

Inventory, 1908

North American Security, Inc.—Item # 453,
Glass Globed Lightning Rod.

Andrew Wyeth, 1950

The object of my visit is antique
as Christina dragging herself across the living
room floor to reach her ladder-back,
sitting hands-in-lap for hours, like history,
like the lightning rod I've come to paint.

The Young Man, 1909

Sitting the ridgepole at Olson's,
putting up the rod, sliding its globe into place,
I see Chrissy shading her eyes, looking up.
That pretty. I'll ask her after work.

The Docent, 2001

Notice how forms in the work are paired:
the tripodal base of the rod and the triangled roof,
the curve of the glass sphere and arc of the bay.
One wonders if Wyeth had another pair in mind:
Christina and Alvaro, brother and sister, keepers
of the house.

Christina Olson, 1950

I like to watch it in a storm—the way it takes
the brunt. As it will today
with weather building, everything fading.
Ten o'clock, already no horizon, the bay vague
in the painting on his easel.

Only the lightning rod is sharp—it always
reminds me of my brother.
But today I'm thinking of the boy up there
and the girl—that night.
I can barely make them out.

EVICTION

I kick the door open. Like a newsreel's
flash of numbers counting down,
followed by the latest from the war zone,
a sudden glare

becomes a sidewalk, traffic, the el.
Small reflection in Eccle the Baker's
window, I'm wearing my Sox cap
over a flyer's leather flaps,

also several coats, both holsters—
all I can take with me.
I aim one finger, thumb cocked,
at everyone staring at the odds

and ends of family—a broken loveseat,
a bureau leaking underwear,
a cracked table covered with maps
riffled by the wind—anywhere

I want to go. A boy is tugged past me
by his mother, she publicly
not looking, he backwards like an owl.
I fire and fire

and something, a mattress,
falls from a third story window,
kicks up a litter of trash—butt ends
and bits of glass.

One end dangles in the gutter.
The ticking is filthy

with stains, some fat and tailed, some
curled like grins.

I fire at these, at the window,
the sky.
And the sidewalk opens—
old Eccle drags a sack the size of me

to the hole,
pushes it in. Scuttle of clawfeet.
The wind rattles the maps—anywhere
I want to go.

ON ASSIGNMENT IN UGANDA

I focus my lens on the boy's upper lip
with its curve and cleft of love's bow
strung with a sweet line of lower lip.

He has turned from the broken wall of
a smoldering church, has taken in what
my camera has shot—hundreds

locked inside, charred
piles of bone sparkling with shards
of stained glass. He knew them.

He holds a sprig of rosemary to
breathe through, sweeten the stench.
It doesn't

keep his lower lip from trembling,
tightening, pulling
away from the bow, beginning

to release a scream. Let it
be shrill enough to shatter the lens
I see through.

ST. GREGORY
OF THE GOLDEN MOUTH

Born on Inis Mór in the Aran Islands, sent to Rome in 398, buried there in 453, transported home when his coffin floated to Cill Rónáin. Not recognized by Rome.

I was so pretty a pagan, the Abbot said, he'd have
me sent to Rome—it was a sin the way I cavorted
from crag to crag in uncured sandals
with the fur still bristling on their soles.

I let myself be sent, hating as I did
the stench of burning dung
that hovered like the Aran fog in small stone rooms
and the beat of the terrible rock-breaking waves

on which the brittle black currachs were tossed
like upended beetles, all six oars flailing.
My own father had been taken by the breakers
at Bungowla, dashed against the rocks and flayed,

brought home in pieces and puzzled together
by three crones keening like the wind
and warning me to kiss his frozen lips or be going
straight to hell.

His father's bones,
bits of gristle clinging, were dug from their patch
of dirt—old poverty of clay and crumbled stone—
for him to be planted in their place

and soon uprooted for the likes of me. I traded that
for the elegance of Rome, where my golden words

elevated me at the Vatican, the Celtic savage
civilized by velvet robes, at home

with the finest the City could offer,
drinking in the sweet marrow of its osso buco
washed down with papal wine. My new ways came
easily. Something lost must have risen in me

the way sweet-water on the Islands,
siphoned off by limestone swallow holes
to carve out underworlds,
will suddenly appear. This lasted thirty years.

I was not prepared, in the midst of Matins,
for the welling up
of Inis Mór's cursive, lacework walls
the early sun shone through, embellishing,

wives waiting on the beach at Cill Mhuirbhigh,
circled in mauve or red by their rings of skirt,
and a stone-gray pony backlit on a crag
above Dún Eochla, mane cresting like the surf.

This morning as I served communion
I saw a coffin lengthen to a currach
bearing my gray and glittering remains
to three islands brightly green on a wine-dark sea.

THE RECTOR'S WIFE

for Elizabeth Rinehart McQuilkin, 1870-1938

How dark it is from the nave to the altar,
how many shades of obsidian, onyx and anthracite
in the black of his robe, and how stark
the white of his collar.

He is giving the sermon.
Behind him, her face a mask the ecru of old lace,
hands sallow as weathered bone, his wife, who once
won the conservatory's Chopin competition,

is at the organ, its ivories like serried rows of
sharp teeth. She believes in redemption,
visits the sick five days a week, calls altar flowers
a form of temptation.

For the short season of these four lines, let her be
among the cosmos, glads and roses she was picking,
flush-faced, humming lieder,
when he came up from his other world.

PENDERGAST'S GARAGE

It's 1940, dusk. There are bats
over Pendergast's Garage, and Mr. P
is polishing a pump.
His black tie is thin and neatly clipped.

Beyond him, rest room signs grow dim—
no Women, no Men. Now lights
illuminate Milky Ways, Mars Bars and
maps of seven states and Essex County.

But a part of the sky is still on fire.
It turns the growth along Pine Road,
to which Mr. P has his back,
red, and deeper red the Flying Horse

big-thighed on the Mobil sign,
which hangs like a flag, and on each
bubble-headed pump and over the heart
of Mr. Pendergast.

He has known the beast to mount,
straight up, the dark
above the thickening trees. And he is
polishing. He sees himself in a pump.

A PAIR OF HOPPERS

1. *"Office at Night," 1940*

Stop putting on airs, sir.
It's not the annual report that keeps you
at your desk so late.
I do.

As you see, Hopper's made improvements
in me. I am, you'll agree, more
bosomed and buttocked.

Don't tell me you don't get it,
the way I ease a file drawer open,
lick a finger, run it down your ridged
folders, and with a sort of pistol

crack
from one high heel, pin
the balance sheet blown off your blotter.

Your options are down to one, mister.
You think there's always the cold mouth-
piece of the phone
to call the wife to say you're on the way?

Fat chance. In no time I'll kneel
to pick up your Profits & Losses and
find your eyes on the dark of my cleavage.

You won't be in any position to tell me
my *Yours Truely* is misspelled.
The only truth is the whisper
of rayon on nylon.

2. "Hotel by a Railroad," 1952

Not satisfied? After thirty years of forgetting I *am*
your wife? Look at you, some stiff
staring out the open window as if it might be just
the ticket.

The few hairs still sticking to your skull are shades
of your threadbare flannels.
The only things not gray about you

are the little red tip of your fag
and those bloodshot eyes squinting at what—
the rails? As if you had the guts to ride them or,
God help you, jump.

So what is it? Let me guess.
You're looking into that opening across the tracks,
thinking

the sun rising precisely between Acme Auto Parts
and the High Meadow Funeral Home
means today's the day for one last adventure.
Some Druid you are!

Button your fly, Don Juan, and settle down.
From here I can see through those
moth-eaten socks

your heels
won't be growing any wings. How dreary the news
of your comings and goings
in the little black book on my lap.

Look, your bed is made. There,
laid out on that pale face of a pillow, mister,
your spectacles.

BRUEGEL'S PLAYERS

How bleak these three who trudge into town
with just one fox to show for the hunt,
their lean dogs slouching behind, heads down,
man and beast black against the sepia snow.

Above, a murder of crows waits patiently.
Only one of the houses sends up any smoke:
the people's firewood has been commandeered
for the Spanish garrison, there,

    against those ice-blue cliffs. But look, oh see,
    says Bruegel, the bliss
    of a magpie sheering the verdigris
    sky, and far below on the sky-green ice, children

skating—such tiny black ciphers enjoying
a touch of carmine for scarf, dot of pink for face.
Three of them chase a fourth; a small boy,
bent-kneed, makes a V

of his blades; another hunches down, spins a top.
Dark stroke, hands muffed, a young woman,
thin from starvation, stops
to watch. She commits the scene to memory.

DANCING AT THE GALLOWS

Beneath gallows designed to put in the Flemish
the fear of an occupying Spanish
God, this spectacle today—such a squealing

of bagpipes, maidens chancing local boys,
and a dozen hogs being slaughtered for the feast,
each given its special Spanish title.

Now a couple of new comers raise the level
of the jig, his codpiece aimed at her lifted skirt
and Spain's posterior. To one side, like the magpie

on the cross-beam of the gibbet (where yesterday
Hans Vander, strangling, kicked his last),
some local wit is occupying a log to take a shit.

CONNEMARA

His well-tuned head is inclined to his fiddle,
eyes shut, features half in the dark
despite a burst of sun. Behind him, Connemara.
In a vale under the fiddle's frets,

the close-up of a crofter's cottage—flayed rafters
of a time-blasted roof, blank sockets of window
and door. And in a briar-tangled graveyard below
Tommy's bow arm, a girl with head back, mouth

open like an entrance to the underworld, howls.
Beyond her, another girl, facing away
toward the village green, holds out her bouquet
to a circle of dancers, their hair flying,

the lichen-scribbled ring of stones around them
fit setting for such tradition.
Farther off, in the bay's wind-blown glitter
at the base of a storm-black ben, a toy ship

sets sail. Tommy's bow saws toward, away from
and toward the ben, a gray road curling out of it
with a black procession of women starkly winding
past a stubborn Norman tower and famine village

toward the ear Tommy bends to his fiddle.
About him spirits crowd. Tiny devils,
charred, grip his waist like moles, staring out as if
to have their picture taken.

Others with the bright-veined wings of damselflies
circle his bow
and tickle the fingers which give such tremolo
to Tommy's tune.

UNFRAMED

WAR NEWS

At breakfast with father
when I grew tired of seeing the war news
on the back of his bare-knuckled
paper, I examined what else stood between us.

For all its British silver, it was Byzantine
and Gallic, onion-domed
and perforated with tiny fleurs-de-lis to
pour the sugar. Or so I say now.

Then, it was merely beyond me. And he went on
flipping pages with angry snaps.
Nothing worth his while there. But still
the paper stayed up,

the test
continued. I thought
of snatching the Times away, finding
my father

less furious
than disappointed I was, as ever,
stupid, stupid, stupid—like all the rest that
passed for news. So I waited,

watched his hand emerge,
huge and graceful,
close gently around the sugar tower,
raise it deftly out of sight behind the paper,

sweeten,
and return it,

49

ridged and shining, to its appointed place.
I made a promise to myself:

I would study harder,
craft myself more perfectly, wait patiently
for him to notice and reach out
that gently to me.

MOVING MOTHER

Every spring she began again
to do her hair, legs curled beneath her,
nude at the heart of the garden,
flush terra cotta, too much the image

of my mother. Not for friends to see.
I was in favor of fall, leaves hiding
parts of her, and at last the removal—
but not the way my father held her

on his way to the cellar, the pitch
black she wintered in—except for one
mica eye of the furnace
blazing, throwing light darkly on her.

What did I know? After he willed her
to me, I took her home
too carelessly, broke off a foot, a hand.

It's time I reconsidered
how she nestled in his arms.

THE LIGHTERS

for my mother

In her eighty-ninth year she's reducing
her inventory—china to the children, mementos
to the trash—but in her boudoir
keeps half a dozen square-shouldered Zippos,

on one her husband's initials,
the best man's on another, the rest anyone's guess.
Dry-chambered, their rusted spark wheels stalled,
they are lined up gravely on a jewelry chest

full of antique gap-toothed keys with elaborate
scrollwork on their hilts, fit to open
high-backed steamer trunks, perhaps the door
to a sunken garden

where every night the dry-bones come
in mothballed flannels and hand-knit sweaters
to roll their own, light up
like fireflies and, sotto voce, remember her.

THE CANE

Knotty, brass-collared, its bone handle
grooved like wrinkled skin,
the eye of a heron at its crook,

her father's cane went everywhere
with her. When airport security
suspected a split in its hickory

hid contraband, she shook it, joyfully
feigned senility,
prevailed.

The less she trusted her pins
the more she trusted the cane to keep her
from a walker or, God help her, wheels.

With it she strode the fairway
of her kitchen, hip-
swinging like her favorite linkster,

and when she took to bed for
good, she kept it close,
would need its support on her journey:

"I have my father's cane,
I have my father's feet,
I am almost there."

She kissed its ivory beak, got a grip on it
below the covers, and when she let go at last
would not let go of it.

ENDANGERED

for my grandson

A tiger is in the tree, William says.
I say it's unlikely: tigers are endangered.

But truly there it is, new wings
spread out to dry, black stripes on yellow,
a tiger swallowtail.

*This is the bad time, a bird may come—
like crossing N. Carefree,* he says,

takes out his paints, makes the butterfly
splay on a cloud as white as cotton batting
in a specimen box.

Under it he puts a leafless tree, one limb
barely supporting a swing. At the bottom
by his name he has written *In Dangered.*

HENRI RAYMOND MARIE DE TOULOUSE-LAUTREC-MONTFA

It wasn't that simple.
Besides Henri and Toulouse and Lautrec
there were those other titles to live up to
and—if you asked Rosa la Rouge
or Madame Poupoule—
some spicy sobriquets as well: Big Spout,
Corkscrew.

So first, Henri,
communicant with certain birds and trees,
a child so beautiful his mother could cry—
the eyes especially, the eyes
in which his thoughts, like bright fish,
moved just below the surface.

Then Raymond—after his uncle the Count
who fell from a horse and died, humped over.
It ran in the family. For no better reason
he fell and broke himself, grew no taller
than a troll. Frog-lipped, enormously nosed,
he made a virtue of stunted limbs,
declared the world to be a circus
and he its dearest freak,
a man the whores would pay to serve.

He'd rise from a night with them
and one or two hours of sleep
to gather his tools, become Marie again
devoted to his copper plates and canvases.

But he never forgot he was a Toulouse
whose people had owned the south of France
and the ear of God. He was born to it,
would tell how his mother kept a bevy of nuns
in one of her chateaus, their only duty
to pray for his sins,
which he was therefore obliged to commit.

He was, after all, Lautrec ("low tricks,"
the envious English quipped). He loved
the drunks, the can-can girls, the aging whores,
was so much a part of the brothel where
he paid handsomely for bed, board and studio
he might have been a gilded ceiling mirror.
Mornings, he stole into their rooms
to sketch the bare-faced ladies before they woke.

At the height of his notoriety, suddenly
no one, Montfa of Montparnasse no more,
he closed up shop, and suffering from
lesions, painful swelling of the testicles and penis
as well as increasing spasms of the hands and feet
and tumors in the brain inducing deafness,

went home.
Curled on the chaise longue at Malromé,
once more Henri, he asked for the songs
his mother had kept in mind for him,
the toy gazelle she'd saved, the silver crucifix.

ARRANGEMENTS IN BLUE & GOLD

1. F. R. Leyland, Tycoon

Jeckyll was my decorator, Whistler my painter,
and neither worth a damn.
One crumpled, the other made a mockery of me.

2. Tom Jeckyll, Decorator

And for the walls, Spanish calfskin
hand-tooled with poppies and pomegranates
brought in by Catherine of Aragon.
Outré, quite perfect.

But not for Whistler. *The colours,* he said,
scream at my painting.
The popinjay! And Leyland
said *Touch it up,* then left for Liverpool
to accrue.

So Whistler painted the calfskin
cobalt blue—and over it, floor to ceiling, peacocks,
gold peacocks flaunting!
It might have been Rossetti's backyard, that zoo.

3. Walter Greaves, Painter's Assistant

The day he heard about young Jeckyll was the
usual. He raged
if a ripple marred the azure I applied.
The peacocks he did himself—

jabbed a brush in gold, sparred with the blue,
touché, touché, and strutted the scaffold,
darting his head from side to side,
monocle in and out, the tips of his moustache
quivering like wings. Then down for a view,
hands spreading behind him.

*Aren't they marvelous,
the fowl?* he crooned, and did his Jeckyll:
*Oh my room, my beautiful beautiful room,
ruined, quite demolished!*

At four the press arrived,
found him lounging, doodling tail feathers
with a brush-tipped fishing pole.
They reported that Jeckyll had gone mad,
painted his bedroom cerulean, gilded
himself, been taken where the walls were soft
enough to keep him from dashing
out his brains, but had managed somehow.

Whistler listened absently,
examined a cuff of his robin's egg suit,
added the yellow kid gloves, the Panama,
the gilt, swan-headed walking stick,
adjusted his lemon cravat,
and thus arranged, flung over his shoulder
Indeed, that is the effect I seem to have.

4. James McNeill Whistler, Artist

The evening was another matter.

Along the plum-blue Thames, the brick kilns
hissed, their red gold fires reflecting

infernally. The tooled sky was navy,
its patterns yellow with age—
like faded poppies and pomegranates.

I vowed no more arrangements
in blue and gold, except for variations on
the night. To this I was true, for several days.

SELF-PORTRAIT AT 14

She stands at her easel,
primed canvas ready
for the self she sees reflected
in fragments

on a pair of gilt French doors.
As little of her as possible
shows. Her eyes are fisted,
dark hair tightly knotted

in a braid as if to lock it in,
overalls baggy, smock
loose as a cassock.
Through herself she sees

a rain-dark garden, at its heart,
kneeling, nude, high-breasted,
this other, undoing her hair
in the midst of glistening laurel.

A sudden infusion of sun
raises the black greens about her
to jaspers and jades.
She is pink as a Veronese.

BAROQUE TIME PIECE

Time was
when time did wonders—
no Alpine lad and lass
darting out and in,
cuckoo, cuckoo,

but whole processions
elaborating
gold-leaved clockworks—
Neptune circumnavigating
hourly, driving dolphins,
eyes rolling like galleons
to see such nereids naked,

and a brazen Eve
biting into a Delicious
on the quarter hour,
in delicto on the half.

WHITTLE

He must have taken his time
as I take mine, late day
on this log. Such a milling of
cedar chips at my feet,

some thin as shed skin,
some thick where his knife
cut hard, and short or lengthy
as he quickened

or mused on what it was
in the cedar
would come to be.
I'd like to think he thought it

trapped in there
like Ariel in the riven pine—
but of course that's me,
not him.

If now I see gray blue wings
easing out of a block of wood
like this morning's heron
out of mist, the mist fills in.

I'm left with shavings
and this: whatever our bent,
whatever hate and love may
curl away from you and me,

not even time, which pares us
aimlessly, can tell what shape
our lives will take—or preordain
a whittle of words.

KACHINA CARVER

Ah, these gods down from the Mount
with their cunning and whimsy, roar
of laughter and anger, incarnation in

dancing dolls this Hopi charmer carves.
True, he keeps up with the competition,
takes shortcuts

courtesy of Hobby USA—its acrylics,
wood burning kit, and Anglo mannikin
he can twist into any position.

But when he's not turning out kachinas
of stunted poplar, legs and arms
glued on for quick sale,

he devotes himself
to those that come from a single
cottonwood root—

down to the very mount on which
the gods are based. At times like these
he and they are of a piece.

SOLSTICE

The lights are out, the fires are cold
in Zuni Pueblo. It is time. Now
across the ice-hard mesa and wash
he comes,

chest and legs dappled red and blue,
blue beads at his wrist and neck,
redtail feather on a white-spotted hood
and over his shoulder a fawn skin

filled with rattling sunflower seed.
He carries a torch against
the dark, and reaches the people,
blesses the hearths,

relights the fires,
dances with the cloud-white, nimbus-
headed, cedar-and-bow-bearing Rain
God of the North. The year begins.

DESERT

Humpbacked with gear and out
of water, I come on the last of
a coyote, eyes lively with maggots.

The buzzards are all
but done. Clack of beak on beak,
a sharpening. The sand burns, rises
about me like the aura of flies
about the coyote.

Around another bend, another,
and there in a recess
low on the canyon wall
rust, white and ochre dancers,
torsos tapering like arrowheads.

Their heads are skulls,
eyes enormous,
robes ornamented with antelope.
Birds occupy their shoulders.
Beside them, snake spirits rise
like walking sticks.

A dust devil spins where I stand
at the foot of the talus
and settles. The heat returns,
the canyon walls resume
their wavering, the dancers repeat
their deliberate step.

The drumming of distant thunder
is just the thrum of a hummingbird

hovering by snakeweed.
I find an alcove in which to be
picked clean—

and wake to wet wind, the scent
of creosote bush, tall clouds rising
over the rimrock, dark as flint.
Lightning flickers, the rain begins.

GHOST RANCH AMPHITHEATER

In this desert of skulls
a cliff raises into white and turquoise sky
a thousand feet of red, beige and yellow stone—

shades of the plastic-flowered, pinwheeled shrines
embellishing the gaudy graveyards
of New Mexico. Such transformation

of death and stone to carnival. And now
where swifts glue debris—snakeskin, rabbitbrush—
to this bandshell of a cliff, making bowls for birth,

what hooting, yipping, baying and cawing
from a band of pueblo kids magnifying themselves,
reverberating, raising their lost lives
by the power of Owl and Coyote and Crow.

CLIMBING THE TOWER

Entering at last the poet's Norman tower
I'm met by a clatter of credit card machines.
Mugs and t-shirts.

A push-button brings in the poet himself
telling of ceremony drowned, rough beasts
on the prowl.

I climb, as archers of William de Burgo
once climbed to shoot Irish peasants
from that embrasure off limits to tourists

where a wing-spread kestrel, in its fort of
broken brush, is tearing the head off a rat,
punching meat in the maws of its rough-
housing young. Keep climbing. And there

beyond the dark stone of the winding stair,
a widening circle of sky,
wildflowers rooting in cracks
of the ramparts—blues, citrons, lavenders
that must have given de Burgo pause
on burnished 13th Century afternoons.

Far off, the seven woods of Coole Park
color in. And below, the Cloon meanders,
reflecting the tower, the rose-purple clouds
and the russet underbelly of a swallow
threading an arch of Butler Bridge.

Now the kestrel from its slot in the tower

splits the sky, blazing device
in a gilding sun—red, blue and buff
rounding into a gyre which tightens
for the kill, but is for now a wild delight.

SAPPHO IN CONCERT

Like any man I am too much shield and spear
to delight her. My pleasure is arranging another
and another nubile audience, setting the stage

for Sappho in concert—that husky alto,
laughter rippling her bared throat, the rush of
blood to her face and arms,

the blur of her fingers on the lyre, then just one
finger trembling, vibrato on the gut
for a chosen one. I wait beyond her boudoir

and when the tongue of love turns to verse,
I take dictation. Time will turn her to fragments
soon enough. I save what I can. This is my love.

AFTER WATERLOO, WHAT

he ordered were parapets of dirt
around the perimeter of his empire at Deadwood
to fend off the madding trade winds and the eyes
of the English, how many thousand English
to keep him in his desert enclave on St. Helena.

Inside the parapets he saw to the installation
of a formal garden sufficient to halt the advance
of an enemy more clever than his witless jailors.

When the hundred peach trees of the promenade
wilted, canaries in the aviary and koi in the pool
keeled, and the pièce de résistance, a brazen
Napoleonic eagle, had the wings hung out to dry
and humpback of a cormorant,

he had to laugh that otherworldly laugh of his.
The worst was the fountain which sputtered like
an old man's seed. He disappeared for days.

But throughout the summer of 1820 guards saw
the bloated Emperor (no one suspected arsenic)
wielding a watering can at 5 a.m.
in his tattered nightgown and dirty red headband.

Barely able to walk, he persisted
in irrigating his pennyroyals, passion flowers
and seven kinds of rose.

He called the first his Marie-Louises, the second

his Josephines, the rest his Little Ladies.
They would never remarry, carried on no affairs,
told no one of his "difficulty." They were all
the forces he had left

to fight the enemy—not the assassin who laced
his white Bordeaux with arsenic, but the sot
who knew the poison by heart and drank it gladly.

UNDER THE SUN

It is warm, unseasonably. Compliant
in the private courtyard of the Emperor
red cyclamen blooms, obsequious and gaudy
as bent-backed courtiers
before His Most Plenipotent & Provident Majesty,

Rudolf II, who herewith emerges to honor
his blood relation, the Sun. Conveyed in pomp
across the Deer Moat and into the Great Hall
to the cadence of an overture
composed for the occasion, he now holds court

below the gold insignium of Helios on the dome
of his sedan. It is his pleasure to receive lesser lights—
goldsmiths, courtesans, poets, painters
and celebrants of science like Magus Tycho Brahe,
Grand Master of Cosmology

now approaching His Majesty, obeisance forgotten.
The Magus, who will die soon of a burst bladder
but whose version of the heavens
is all the rage,
arranges himself to deliver an oration.

He declares the Emperor to be Earth
around which the Sun and its entourage turn.
And who must be the Sun
but Magus Tycho Brahe! His nose portends it,
he notes, meaning his stunning proboscis,

prosthesis of gold whose aquiline forebear was

lopped off in a duel. As he turns to face
Arcimboldo's portrait of Rudolf, collation of
fruits and vegetables in which the Imperial nose
is but a ruddy pear,

the only sound is the click of the cosmologist's
jeweled hand on his 24-karat schnozz.
Slowly he begins his ceremonial orbit
of the throne, and direly the Scion of the Sun
rises, brings down his sword on Master Brahe

to dub him.
Stop here, with the Emperor's sense of irony
intact, the Imperial Master of Cosmology sure
of his distinction, no bubbles burst,
no war of religion today.

AN ASTONISHMENT AND AN HISSING

*Babylon shall become heaps, a dwelling place for dragons,
an astonishment and an hissing, without an inhabitant.*
                                                —Jeremiah, 51

And it was as the hand had written on her wall:
the Jewel of the East, Lady of Two Rivers,
Ark of Ishtar and Marduk—Babylon

was dust. The wonder of her gardens hung to veil
too fragrant communion from the jealous gods,
her Tower of Towers,

the manacled dragons inlaid along her avenues
and sculpted kings brazen as the bulging sun
that crouched behind the Tigris,

her myriad victories
carved in ivory set in lapis lazuli—all were broken,
all burned.

After the pitch that bound her bricks
ran boiling in the streets, and golden gods, gone
molten, flowed in channels carved for blood,

after the perfumed cedar of ceilings cooled to ash
and even Alexander, kicking through the rubble,
grew weak at the thought of raising her again—

after her shame was all the world could wish,
Jehovah wished more, uncoiled long muscles
and sinuous as script, slid into her, hissing.

In the end the brown-voiced Euphrates

and wailing siroccos
buried her under centuries of silt and sand,

buried all but the ghost of Nebuchadnezzar.
Ox-bodied, vulture-clawed, he crawls
the desert over Babylon.

RETROSPECTIVE

for Sarah

So many takes of Jo at this retrospective
(they say he married her for a permanent model)—
Jo as hooker, nipples rouged, hair flaming with
henna, Jo hunched at a counter, night hawking,
Jo as wolf girl crawling into bed, nether fur licked
by the lecherous wind,
or naked at a gaping flophouse window.

Once, happily, she's Pierrette,
white ruff at neck and wrists, receiving applause
she deflects with a deprecating gesture of her hand
toward Pierrot, clearly Hopper himself
who touches his chest
as if before he can bring himself to respond

he feels an old weakness of the heart
keep him remote as the coast of Maine he loves
the way she wishes to be loved, wishes
so terribly she rages.
I understand. I too have earned such rage
though you keep it to yourself, my dear, as we go on
from Hopper to Hopper.

Now from a dark place behind *Two Comedians*
where a film shows every half hour,
a loud thud
is followed by strange soprano laughter,
not laughter—the ascending laceration of a scream
rising into a gasped series of *No's*,

then the silence that follows a natural disaster.

Across the gallery your face is unmasked
in a shock so pure
it's a mirror for mine. How long
it has been since we looked at each other
so, not husband, not wife,
but true as only strangers thrown together are.

ADVENT CALENDAR

At the dark end of the year
when the owl sweet talks
all night, I pause before
the final door

of an Advent calendar, wait to
look in on the child. Let's hope
I'm not a spy, house to house,
for Herod, or that if I am

I'll quit the service
when I find what I want.
Now the sweet talk quickens
to silence. What murder is on

the wing? I look for signs of it
in myself, who have no gift for
him, but will not turn away.
I try the door.

GETAWAY

after an early work by Mack Burns, age 3

He crayoned his first crèche in three parts.
All's well at the top—the Firmament is
heavenly blue. But the Sky
is trouble. It's full of what—stars or angels
swarming like a plague of leggy spiders.

Just above the manger is a star burst
from something like a Scud
incoming. Part Three has the Baby Jesus
the size of his parents, his feet and head
protruding from a purple perambulator.

A lush brown, black-haired Mary,
her arms and one leg colored jaggedly,
leans forward as if to wheel the giant baby,
hissing to the blueblood blob of Joseph
Let's get out of here!

The space around the shed is fire-orange
except for a—camel? Brown as Mary
and humped high as the ridgepole,
it's kicking a hole in the siding. To knock
sense into Joseph's head? Or show it's

raring to go? Maybe left by a Wise Man
after he informed on the king. But—
shouldn't it be a donkey? A minor mistake.
Thank God for its headstrong headful
of a stall somewhere Herod never heard of.

THE CRY

Below a banner proclaiming the museum's Rodin exhibit,
this outdoor sculpture so exact it is almost alive:
a beige-and-white-striped hawk, eyes glaring, razor beak
aimed at me. It is mounted

on a buff and blue and iridescent pigeon, in which
its talons are dearly sunk. Now this—the hawk blinks once,
a switchblade's click. Nothing else moves. Not the pigeon,
not I.

I admire such art, the ripple of muscle
as the Redtail shifts its weight, raises one leg, digs in
more deeply.

I admire. Still—yesterday, a block away, another drive-by.
World, world, so much bad blood.
I feel the thud, the talons striking bone, the quick cry
rising in my gorge.

MERRY GO ROUND
AT THE WADSWORTH ATHENEUM

Hartford, 1973

A museum is not a circus!
he says, pointing to the newest installation
he's paid to guard,

to wit, these painted ponies in Avery Court,
teeth bared, ears back,
lacquered fuchsia, orange, blue, chartreuse

from a fin de siècle carousel in Troy, N.Y.
They're half inclined
to paw the well-rounded Venus they circle.

And now in the city of Stevens, how aptly
the guard's *tsk-tsking* quickens to
a trot, his jingle of keys to a clatter of tack

as he vaults on the one with a violet mane
and gleefully, in time to so much
organ-grinding,

gets going
up, down and merrily round the goddess.
She's delighted to see him lean so far

out like anyone after the brazen ring,
heart going like her own,
that Wurlitzer.

TEN

for Matt and Nicole

Her brother builds the solar system
out of styrofoam, remote, not talking.
The planets are mostly done, brightly
attached to the sun, the rings of Saturn
in the works on a pasteboard brim.

Her answer is her mother's
abalone shell comb, pink jade earrings,
malachite pendant coiled to strike,
ruby, turquoise, sapphire rings
and cincture of green glass beads.

She jingles into the moonstone night,
stands unsure,
then slowly, then faster, begins to spin
around herself.

INVITATION

Mother has shown me the secret
bowl of twigs and twine,
snake skin, horse hair and rabbit fur
in forsythia
trimmed like a hood.

From here, waxwings,
expecting, sang all April
their yellow, tawny, crested songs.
They were mistaken.
They left.

She's careful to leave a gap
in the forsythia for their return
and in herself another
for whoever she was when she was
at home in herself, a schoolgirl

skating, polka dotted clown suit
billowing, huge ruffles at the neck,
one leg in the air like a tail,
arms out for balance, head cocked
to sing.

DISCOVERY

In a shot of my parents courting, spring vac at Oxford,
the sun illuminates my handsome father, casts the bulk
of his shadow on my mother, who all but disappears.
Which is how it was when I came into the picture.

Only years later, after he went under, did she begin—
only then could I see—
Let me put it this way: perhaps you know
about the Villa of the Lost Papyri in Herculaneum,

those arcades, fountains, mosaics, stunning
trove of marble nudes, obsidian busts with jade and
   ivory eyes.
We understand now, of course, that the true treasure
was hidden deep in dark archives.

When archaeologists unearthed the villa, buried by
   Vesuvius,
they puzzled over thousands of cylinders dark as coal,
burned some against the cold, kept hunting for treasure
until one day someone noticed characters inscribed in
   the char.

As the cylinders were slowly unraveled, there it was
on papyri all but destroyed but in the end preserved by
   disaster:
lost philosophy, drama, poetry of another world
a curator recorded, swiftly, before it could disintegrate.
I would, dear mother, do no less for you.

WORK IN PROGRESS

for Norah Pollard

Her reply to the wreckage of his body
pocked by needles & stubbed-out smokes

is this sharp-clawed red & gold bird
she jabs to life with angry stabs of acrylic.

She makes & makes the fabulous thing
rise raging from its pyre.

LADDERS TO GLORY

The drawbridge grinds its gears,
leans on the sky, a kind of ladder.
Its rungs—well, see for yourself
how well versed those I-beams are

in row on row of—not smut
but what anyone with a ten-inch
brush and a gallon of Glidden
would inscribe at high tide

on something bound to rear up
so religiously: Day Glo billets doux
in script a full foot tall. SC does
it, I'm glad to hear. But just now
I'm pushing into open water—

Look, through the cumulus
a ladder of light is being lowered.
Gulls ascend and descend it.
Glad you feel that way up there.
I'll do my best.

WRITER'S GUIDE

EKPHRASIS

The poems in *Private Collection* are based on many kinds of art from painting and sculpture to graffiti, crayon drawings and snapshots. They reflect a belief that art is at least as "real" as anything in our lives and that *ekphrasis* (translation of art to literature) is a liberating experience.

Ekphrasis allows a writer to create an impression rather than a description, adding personal and philosophical dimensions to an artwork, subtracting from and adding to it as necessary, always seeing it as a starting point, not an end-all. Ekphrasis also allows for showing other "frames" before and after an artwork—in a sort of cinematic sequence. At the same time, close observation of a static work of art is often the key to finding the poem implicit in it. Considerations such as these as well as other suggestions for your own writing will be found in the notes that follow, each of which contains one or more writing topics.

To help you *see* the relationship of art to poetry, the notes provide information on art alluded to by the poems and suggest that to view it (or related poems) you should explore the internet, where many works of art and literature are available. Submitting a creator's name and/or the title of a work to a search engine such as Google will often produce a display of the work as well as background information. Whenever possible, specific websites have been suggested. In some cases, sites may have disappeared or changed their offerings, but new material is constantly being added to the internet. Items currently available on-line are marked with an asterisk.

The notes also comment on the poems and suggest topics for discussion—in a classroom, book group, or the inner sanctum of your mind. Other notes as well as poetry written in response to assignments will be posted on the seminar page of the Antrim House website (www.antrimhousebooks.com), along with artwork not available elsewhere on the internet.

THE ART OF IT

There is an art to the reading of poetry. A poem is not an editorial. It should be read *slowly* and several times: like a person worth knowing, it will reveal itself gradually. And some of what it has to say will reside in its sound. *Listen* to it. Because we are not a patient people, poetry often exasperates us. Given a chance, however, it can be the news we need.

Now a few thoughts on the art of writing poetry. A promising poem will have a mind of its own; your role as a writer is to understand that mind and follow its lead. At the same time you need to keep Pegasus under control. In particular, you should practice the art of *cinching:* removal of unnecessary explanations that tell the reader what to think, often adjectives and adverbs stealing thunder from nouns and verbs, bloating one's writing and making it seem merely words, words, words.

Writing which consists primarily of nouns and verbs is muscular, liable to stress images rather than explanations, and that is precisely what we should be after as writers. The art is to present the facts and let the reader supply the explanations. Hemingway knew this well. Having cinched *The Old Man and the Sea*, stressing nouns and verbs, he created a story rich in sight, sound, smell, taste and touch; the images speak for themselves, without commentary. When we finish the book, our hands are raw from fighting sharks. We feel, therefore we think.

In selecting nouns and verbs, you might want to opt for the Anglo-Saxon, monosyllabic choices rather than the more elaborate Latinate ones. A *kiss* is better than an *osculation*. Simplify, simplify, as Strunk and White tell us in *The Elements of Style*. And strive for clarity. 'Tis a gift not to write the incomprehensible gibberish that sometimes passes for poetry in academia.

A note on titles. They are the handles of your poems, and therefore vital. True, providing no title at all is better than providing a poor one. But a good title, especially one that cuts in at least two complementary directions, offers an entry into the life of a poem.

Caveat: avoid titles which are overly explanatory or insult the reader's intelligence. And remember Samuel Johnson's dictum that the writer should delete whatever is overly clever.

Revision has an unfortunate reputation. It can be an exciting process, letting a writer come closer to the marrow of an idea and discover truths that might not have been clear to him or her before. I once wrote a poem in which my father, as a young boy, looks up from a front row pew to see his terrifying rector of a father breaking the wafer during communion. In the first version, the boy imagined he was the broken wafer. In revising the poem, I realized that the real truth was far more dire. The newer version reads like this:

Like Abraham with Isaac overhead, you held the Host,
then broke it. The wafer, snapping, might have been
me, held up, an example. Of course it wasn't.
It was God. Over and over, God broke
beneath your hands.

The revision crossed in the mail with a rejection from *Poetry*, which reversed its decision in light of the change. More importantly, I had discovered the full import of the poem, had delved more deeply.

All that having been said, it remains true that the best words come spontaneously. Good poetry tends to write itself and surprise the poet. After a wild ride, however, your poem may need some attention. Be a bold rider and a good groom.

Now on to some thoughts concerning the poems in this volume, along with writing topics to which they lead.

NOTES

Page 13: Dioramas are fascinating in the way the actual merges with the virtual in them—a real tree limb joins its painted extension on a backdrop, half a split stone is completed by its acrylic partner. The seam where one meets the other is much like the place between dream and dailyness where "real toads" inhabit "imaginary gardens," the place of poetry, according to Marianne Moore. Memorable art, too, has a way of being both earthly and unearthly.

Writing: a) One of the best remedies for writer's block is visiting museums of natural history, nature centers, or even internet wildlife sites such as www.enature.com. After doing so, write about the relationship between what is "natural" and what is mounted or replicated, even if the former consists only of your fingers on the keyboard. b) Write about the interaction between any display and those observing it (store-front mannikins and sidewalk gawkers, a model railway setup and its operator, a doll house and the doll house keeper). See cummings' "spring is like a perhaps hand." * (available on the internet)

Page 14: This poem arose from a life-long fascination with the works of Andrew Wyeth, which often draw attention to their real subjects by indirection. "Distant Thunder,"* "Hay Ledge,"* and "Christina's World"* are interesting examples. Wyeth's artfulness teaches us that the most vivid and interesting way to make a point is to imply. For a writer, this might mean creating a parable rather than a sermon. As Emily Dickinson said, "Tell all the Truth but tell it slant."

Sources: "Distant Thunder (tempera), 1961, private collection; "Hay Ledge" (tempera), 1957, private collection; "Christina's World" (tempera), 1948, The Museum of Modern Art, New York.

Writing: Base a poem on an artistic series—Vermeer's servants, Bruegel's peasants, Wyeth's Helga paintings, etc. Do not distrust research. A key fact or two may be crucial. My own research for "In Wyeth" turned up interesting information that is reflected here and in another "Wyeth poem" (p. 33). A web-search will be helpful for Vermeer, Bruegel and other artists, although less so for Wyeth. Some of his works can be seen at www.artbrokerage.com and www.artchive.com. Also try a Google search.

Page 15: The photograph which inspired this poem is delightful partly because of its combination of formality and freedom—bowlers and vests vs. the wild ride to come. Though intent on kicking up its heels, the poem also called for formality and began to emerge in loosely rhyming couplets. Such a contrast can add torque, as when Theodore Roethke combines control and abandon in a poem like "My Papa's Waltz,"* with its rollicking bedtime ride cradled by a traditional a-b-a-b/ c-d-c-d rhyme scheme.

Source: "Plaisir d'Hiver," daguerreotype by an unknown French photographer, late 19th Century.

Writing: Choose a work of folk art (e.g., a Currier & Ives,* a Grandma Moses,* a 19th Century daguerreotype) and write a formal, rhymed poem based on it, trying to make the poem as uncivilized in content as it is civilized in form. For traditional poetic forms, web-search "Poetic Forms."

Page 19: This poem arose from close observation. An almost imperceptible spurt of ice from one of the Reverend's skates and the faint outline of an early version of his hat set the poem in motion. It seemed to compose itself, and I never saw the finale coming until I found myself writing it. That sort of ending can be trusted.

Source: "The Rev. Robert Walker Skating on Duddingston Loch" (oil on canvas), Sir Henry Raeburn, c. 1794, National Gallery, Edinburgh, Scotland. For a reproduction, see www.abcgallery.com.

Writing: Get out your magnifying glass. Look closely for the telling details in an artwork depicting action of some sort (a sporting event, a disaster, an escape), especially those details which point in thematic directions. One of them may act like the heart of a snowball. Roll it. Winslow Homer* is one artist whose work often features action. For inspiration, see how W.H. Auden used details in Bruegel's "The Fall of Icarus" to guide him in the writing of "Musée des Beaux Arts." (A web-search citing author, artist and titles will unearth very useful information.)

Page 21: Imagining nuns in un-nunlike situations has always intrigued me: a nun as locomotive engineer, a nun in the finals at Wimbleton. Thus, when I came upon "The Badminton Game" at the Tate, I consecrated two proper young women bandying a birdie in their graceful Georgian setting. Surely they should have been nuns and the pale daylight moon above them called for Vespers.

Seeing through the mind's eye of the central character was helpful in writing the poem: when Sister's cry hovered in the sky overhead, I imagined her sighting through the gut of her racket, which transformed the cry into a shuttlecock.

Let your senses have a field day when bringing a painting to life. In this case, despite the Georgian silence of the scene, I tried to hear the slightest sounds. It can also help to make a still shot a motion picture, as when Sister "goes back for a long one..."

An interesting sidelight: this poem, having begun with a painting, was translated back into two prints when it was published. One appeared when the poem was first issued in book form; in it, Sister's opponent has a skeletal face—like Death herself. Earlier, when the poem appeared in *The Atlantic Monthly*, it was accompanied by a whimsical Edward Gorey illustration. Two entirely different readings of the poem and both, I suppose, right.

Source: "The Badminton Game," David Inshaw (oil on canvas), 1972-3, Tate Gallery, London. See www.tate.org.uk.

Writing: Compose a poem which transposes identities in an artwork. In a depiction of Leda and the Swan, for instance, Leda might be a Westport housewife or you yourself. Don't be afraid of changing other elements in your art of choice: try for an impression, not a depiction. You may want to describe events through the eyes of a character in your poem (e.g., the Swan).

Page 23: The key to writing this poem was, as ever, close observation. When the narrator says "Look again," he is speaking from experience, having looked closely at details such as a dimly visible coven of crows. Also key was establishing an angle of vision. In this case, there are two observers of the painting, the second of whom makes a surprise entrance and does something which is perhaps as much a surprise to him as it was to the poet.

The original version ended with the red-scarved lady insisting on festivity. In revision, this seemed too pretty, too pat. The lines I added at that point were these: "He wishes her well/ against the clenching sky, the crows." Revision can toughen a poem.

Source: "Sleigh Ride" (oil on canvas), Winslow Homer, c. 1893, Clark Art Institute, Williamstown, Massachusetts. See "Community Webshots" via a Google web-search (enter artist and title in the search box).

Writing: Try a poem in which a work of art is just being conceived, started or finished. For instance, you might begin when Leonardo da Vinci is adding the final touches to that famous smile. Some research could help; in this case, it might lead to a flashback. For me, research is a joy in itself. Do not hurry the process, and by all means take your time when revisiting and revising your poem.

Page 24: True to its 19th Century origins, this poem is formal with its mythical underpinning, its repetitive rhyme scheme, and its allusions to Keats and Yeats (see "Ode on a Grecian Urn"* and "The Second Coming"*). If the poem does its job, however, a rough beast is loose within its formal confines.

Source: "The Stonebreaker" (oil on canvas), Gustav Courbet, 1857-1858, Memorial Art Gallery, Rochester, NY. See www.artcyclopedia.com (Courbet/Memorial Art Gallery). Because the reproduction is very dark, you may have trouble seeing the small patch of sky in the upper right, but enlargement will help.

Writing: Most works of art are frozen in time. Depict one in its time-stopped form, but at the very end set it in motion, either forward or backward. Example: an apparently placid model (e.g., Wyeth's Helga*) might interrupt her pose in an unexpected way; or the death depicted in an artwork (e.g., Goya's "Execution of the Rebels of the 3rd of May"*) might undo itself, moving sequentially backward to a more peaceful time, as far back as you wish to take it.

Page 25: When I began this poem, I had only a general idea of where it might be headed. For many years I'd lived with the photograph on which it is based, but until I became involved in the poem, I was not fully aware of the arch in Eve's eyebrow or the serpentine shape on which her head is leaning and to which she seems to listen. Nor had the crack in her wrist ever seemed more than the sign of a cathedral's monumental shifting. Her Molly Bloomesque *yes yes yes* also surprised me. When I began a line with a single *yes* in the narrator's voice, I wasn't ready for it to become Eve's triple-tongued cry. Which is to say that after sufficient preparation a writer should plunge into the making of a poem with faith that it will take on a life of its own. Be patient and stay with it. One thing will lead to another.

In the first version of the poem, the fifth and sixth lines read thus: "...Nonchalantly,/ she reaches for another apple." For me, "as if to scratch" is more graphic than "nonchalantly," and an anachronistic Winesap is more evocative than a generically biblical apple. Specifics, specifics.

Source: a frieze panel in the Cathedral of St. Lazare, located in Autun, France. See the back cover for a replica. Other images of carvings from the same cathedral can be seen on the internet.

Writing: Compose a love poem (perhaps ambivalent, as in the model) addressed to any character in a work of art. The speaker might be you or someone else. Don't assume you know all the secrets of your poem, most of all the ending. Allow those secrets to reveal themselves.

Page 26: The painting behind this poem is more sensual than most of Homer's work and no doubt shocked him; hence his alleged attempt to tidy it up.

Source: "A Summer Night" (oil on canvas), Winslow Homer, 1890, Musée d'Orsay, Paris. See www. artchive.com.

Writing: a) Become a character in an artwork of your choice, not necessarily a major character, and address the artist, the viewer, or another person in the painting.

b) You might try crawling into the world of an artwork, immersing yourself in it and describing the unexpected nooks you find. But be careful not to get lost in there like Billy Collins, who lit out for the "hills and flowing water" of a Hudson River landscape and was never seen again ("The Brooklyn Museum of Art" in *The Apple that Astonished Paris*).

c) Collins is a memorable ekphrasist. Read "Student of Clouds," "Candle Hat," "Mappamundi," "Putti in the Night," and "Instructions to the Artist" (*Questions about Angels*); "Metropolis" (*The Art of Drowning*); "Fishing on the Susquehanna in July," "Victoria's Secret" and "Musée des Beaux Art Revisited" (*Picnic, Lighting*). A web-search will lead you to some of the above. After a journey in poems like these, it is difficult not to "do a Collins." Give in to the impulse.

Page 27: I was helped by seeing the dim outline of a factory in the background of the photograph on which this poem is based. It seems to represent (or be) the world from which the lovers have escaped. Another breakthrough came from hearing with my inner ear. The man is humming.

Source: Untitled photograph, Gilles Peress, *Paris Magnum,* p. 101, Magnum Photos, Inc., New York and Paris, 1981 (not available on the internet).

Writing: Compose a love poem based on any unconventional pairing of lovers in a work of art. Look and listen carefully. Remember the other three senses as well.

Page 28: An approach for a poem on "Baptism in Kansas" didn't suggest itself until I viewed the scene through the eyes of a minor character in the painting, a young boy standing in a group of adults. As soon as I began to write from his point of view, *a local habitation and a name* followed, and the poem began to write itself. Having no idea how it would end, I let Ellen McGee come up from the water trough and watched what happened. (Grace Paley is right: a story is always smarter than the story-teller.) As ever, revision was indispensable. The first draft was badly overwritten. Rather than limiting itself to "her face was where the sun had been," for instance, it tried to describe the aura about Ellen's face. Bad idea. Leave room for the imagination.

Source: "Baptism in Kansas" (oil on canvas), John Steuart Curry, 1928, Whitney Museum of American Art, New York, NY. See www.gardenofpraise.com.

Writing: View the works of painters in the American Regionalist school—Grant Wood, Thomas Hart Benton, John Steuart Curry, et al.* Those works are full of narrative potential and will lead to interesting poetry. Just as "Baptism" turns a motionless image into a motion picture, your poem might show the before and after of the artwork on which it is based. Also remember that an angle of vision is important.

Page 30: This poem is based on an Eighteenth Century Japanese print entitled "Giant Snowball." In it, four young women in colorful kimonos are rolling snow in a Japanese garden, making an enormous pink-white snowball. On a platform above, lounging in an open-sided teahouse, are two older, blank-faced matrons looking down impassively. Off to the side is a stream in which a pair of mandarin ducks preen. It is a strange, almost comic scene, but haunting and colored extravagantly. The print inspired research into the culture of geishas, including their ritual indoctrination. The poem that followed has a different tone from the print and lacks five of its six characters. Still, the snow is rolled, the mandarins shine, and the powers that be are just off stage. The print was a catalyst but not a confinement.

Source: "Giant Snowball" (ink, colors and gold on paper), Japanese (Tosa school), 18th Century, from an album illustrating *The Tale of Genji,* Metropolitan Museum of Art, New York. Not available on-line.

Writing: Find a photograph or painting depicting a subculture (from the circus, a religion, a trade, etc.) and learn all you can about that subculture. Let what you have learned find its way into a poem. Write with your ears open. Different sorts of sound are appropriate for different sorts of poems (e.g., a jackhammering rhythm and hard consonants for a poem describing the tunnel-makers of New York).

Page 32: Having discovered that Pieter de Hooch created his checkered floors before painting his characters, I wondered how the de Hooch that inspired this poem must have looked as it evolved on the easel. I also wondered about the characters. Like all of de Hooch's young women, the one in the painting at hand is full of mystery. Perhaps if I wrote her into a poem, I thought, I would learn something about her.

The rather unconventional rhyme scheme of this poem began to develop on its own. For that reason and because of the poem's formal content, I urged rhyme in the direction it had in mind, allowing partial as well as full rhyme, the better to keep it unobtrusive. For me, that's the way end-rhyme emerges: only when it has a mind to. Internal rhyme, however, is less particular.

Source: "A Woman Drinking with Two Men and a Serving Woman" (oil on canvas), Pieter de Hooch, c. 1658, National Gallery,

London. See www.kfki.hu (under Collections/web gallery of art/ de Hooch/3rd page).

Writing: Like the American Regionalists, the Dutch and Flemish masters are poets' painters. Immerse yourself in works by one of them: Vermeer, deHooch, Hals, Rembrandt, Bruegel the Elder, et al.* Biographical facts and painting habits (use of the *camera obscura,* for instance) may be useful. Practice *negative capability:* don't fret if you don't know exactly where your research is headed, since poetry is bound to come of it, not to mention joy. Your poem too will be all the more interesting if you can't predict it entirely. Should it show an inclination to rhyme when it emerges, help it out.

Page 33: Research enriched this poem, revealing biographical facts such as the way Christina Olson (a polio victim) was forced to drag herself on all fours, leaving a trail in the dust wherever she went in her house. Her early love affair, however, is an invention. I hope it touches on an essential truth.

Source: "Northern Point" (tempera), Andrew Wyeth, 1950, Wadsworth Atheneum, Hartford, CT. For a replica see www.artbrokerage.com (under "12 Wyeth Classified Listings").

Writing: Compose a poem that circles about an artwork and looks at it from several points of view: those of the artist, outside observers, people/animals in or related to the work... The more diverse the points of view, the more energy your poem will have. For another example, see "Arrangements in Blue & Gold," p. 57. This technique might be called *literary cubism.*

Page 35: I wish I could locate the source of this poem: the photograph of a boy dressed in many layers and standing in the midst of family belongings on a city sidewalk. In looking at it as a possible poem, I found myself reverting to my own painful youth, and the child in me went forth to become this other child, despite a number of differences between us. This freed me to write in a new way.

Writing: Adopting the point of view and voice of someone unlike yourself in age, background and/or gender is one of the surest ways to unleash your genie. Having imagined himself into Huck Finn, Mark Twain began to write with new energy; the same is true of Salinger with Holden Caufield and Wally Lamb with Dolores Price in *She's Come Undone.* Try a poem in which you adopt the voice of someone in an artwork, preferably someone quite different from you. If the art is static, consider turning it into a cinematic sequence, as "Eviction" does by starting a frame or two before the photograph at hand and going several frames beyond it.

Page 37: It was only as I revised and began to envision a new ending that I understood this poem wanted to focus on the photographer as much as on the boy who is his subject. I nudged the poem in that direction, for instance substituting "what my camera has shot" for "what my camera has seen."

Source: *Newsweek* photograph, April 3, 2000, Peter Andrews, Reuters.

Writing: Keep an eye out for arresting photos and clips in news reports. Translate one of them into a poem, remembering that what you think the poem is about may not be what *it* has in mind. In revision you may come closer to that, which is to say closer to your own deepest feelings.

Page 38: When I was in a small church on Inishmaan, the least traveled of the three Aran Islands, I saw a marvelous stained glass window. The day was gray, but the reds, greens, golds and indigos of the window were so vibrant that sun seemed to be pouring through. One of the panels showed a man bearing a bishop's regalia, arms crossed on his chest, lying in a sort of box-boat. Across the waters were three humped backs of what might have been whales—or islands. Next day, a friend told me the story the panel depicted. It was too legendary not to write about and seemed to call for a ballad-like narrative full of memories accumulated during my stay on the honeycombed Arans. For additional Aran Island background, I read John Millington Synge's *The Aran Islands*.

Source: Stained glass window by Harry Clarke in Kilcanonagh Chapel on Inishmaan (Inis Meáin). No image of the window itself is available, but the island itself is well represented on-line.

Writing: A search of the internet will lead you to paintings and other works of art derived from mythical, legendary and biblical sources. Base a narrative poem on one of them. Flesh out the story you create, filling it with the reality of fact—things seen, heard, smelled, tasted and touched. Let it seem to have happened just yesterday, and consider making the speaker one of the characters.

Page 40: One of Robert Marx's eerie oils (such variations on black and white) took me back to the lives of my father's mother and her starkly Presbyterian pastor of a husband. She, whom I had never met, materialized as I wrote "The Rector's Wife." Her story, which had always troubled me, would not have emerged without the help of the Marx painting. The arts are powerful stimuli for one another. There are poems and stories locked inside us all, just waiting for the right catalyst, perhaps a painting, film, sculpture or photograph. As always, in composing this poem I allowed the *sound* of words to have some say in the way they followed one another.

Source: The title of the Marx oil painting that inspired this poem is unknown. It was exhibited at a gallery in Rochester, NY, c. 1994.

Writing: "The Rector's Wife" has my grandparents in the roles of Persephone and Hades. Try repeating the last assignment, this time including members of your own family in the cast of your "myth-poem."

Page 41: Again, I want to underscore the value of careful observation. You never know how an apparently unimportant detail may give direction to a poem. In this case, I noticed that a restroom sign in Hopper's "Gas" is darkened to a rectagular shape without characters. Thus "no Women, no Men." It also helps to enter a work of art in order to see it from within and from a variety of perspectives. In mulling "Pendergast's Garage," I wandered into the office of the filling station and came back out so I could see Mr. Pendergast from a different angle. I also imagined my way back into his earlier life. The more I roamed, the closer I came to the heart of the poem.

Source: "Gas" (oil on canvas), Edward Hopper, 1940, Museum of Modern Art, New York. See www.artchive.com.

Writing: Hopper's work is full of poetic potential. All that gorgeous light and architecture, all those isolated, lonely people. A web search will reveal many of his paintings and much information on his life. As you examine Hopper's work and life, watch for the germ of a poem.

Page 42: It is interesting to think of an artist's paintings as interconnected. In this poem I have linked two of Hopper's works, the younger man in the first becoming an earlier incarnation of the older man in the second. The two women in the paintings are opposite in some ways and similar in one. Adopting their voices gave the poem a Thurber-like thrust.

Sources: "Office at Night" (oil on canvas), Edward Hopper, 1940, Walker Art Center, Minneapolis; "Hotel by a Railroad" (oil on canvas), Edward Hopper, 1952, Joseph H. Hirshhorn Foundation. For a replica of "Office at Night" see www. webshots.com (choose "Community" and enter painter/title in the search box). For "Hotel by a Railroad" there are several depictions on the web.

Writing: a) Find two paintings, photographs, busts, or cartoons of the same person at different times or in different places, and depict that doubled person: a child and the courtesan she becomes, Clark Kent and Superman. The central characters might speak for themselves, or the speaker could be an observor (say, a confused Lois Lane). b) As an alternative, you might create a conversation or confrontation between dissimilar portraits (Rembrandt as a young man and an elder, younger and older incarnations of a celebrity such as Judy Garland, Road Runner before and Road Runner after a run-in with Wily Coyote).

Page 44: Composing a poem based on Bruegel's "The Hunters in the Snow" was a daunting prospect, given the number of poems (six that I know of) inspired by the painting, in particular John Berryman's well-known early poem, "Winter Landscape."* What gave me courage was some interesting research suggesting that the painting, like many of Bruegel's, has political implications. The occupation of the Netherlands by Spanish troops, which caused starvation, persecution and other hardships, outraged Lowlanders such as Bruegel. Looking at the painting in that light led me to notice the military garrison in the distance as well as many indirect signs of occupation (even the tavern sign is dangling askew). The hunters trudging home with only one fox to show for their trouble, then, become symbolic of a larger problem, as does the lack of chimney smoke. The merrymaking on distant ice can also be seen in a new light. As ever, holding a magnifying glass to the painting and to the history behind it was a great help, both in writing the poem and in understanding that a political painting—or poem—need not wear its *P* on its sleeve.

Source: "The Hunters in the Snow" (oil on wood panel), Pieter Bruegel the Elder, 1565, Kunsthistorisches Museum, Vienna. (Note that Bruegel the Elder removed the "h" from his name as a nationalistic gesture.)

Writing: Base a poem on an artwork showing the ravages of war, occupation or despotism (perhaps a painting by Goya or a photograph by Matthew Brady, Henri Cartier-Bresson, Gilles Peress, Margaret Bourke-White, Robert Capa, Eddie Adams or David Turnley, all of whom can be found on-line). Such ravages might be shown indirectly as well as directly. Perhaps there will be room for the uprising of joy in the midst of it all. Avoid overt statements that *tell* what you feel; rather, rely on description. If in doubt, understate. Let the reader come to his or her own conclusions.

Page 45: The line break at the end of the first stanza may be of interest, as may the mix of fact and fiction in this poem. Several details have been conjured, including the pig roast and Hans Vander's hanging. These are, as it were, *imaginary toads in a real garden.*

Source: Pieter Bruegel the Elder, "Magpie on the Gallows," 1568, Hessisches Landesmuseum. For a replica, visit www.mystudios.com. or www.elibron.com (choose Elibron Art Gallery).

Writing: Compose a poem based on a work of art which shows resilience or courage in the face of hardship. You might look for photographs depicting wartime conditions (see last assignment) or areas of the world, including the USA, where times are hard. Consider the work of photographer Walker Evans and WPA images from the Depression years,* as well as photos of recent disasters. See what can be accomplished with line breaks, and don't be afraid of adding/changing details.

Page 46: The painting behind this poem is so rich in image and symbol that the poem differs from most of the others in being pure (though selective) description. The attempt here was to stress the painting's dualities, with an eye to the universal truth they embody. It also seemed important to replicate the painting's richness of image, find language sufficient to the occasion, and sustain an emerging rhyme scheme.

Source: "Tommy's Music/The Source" (oil on canvas), by Catharine Kingcome, 1977. See www.irishfiddle.com/art (tommysmusic). A web-search will bring up other works by Kingcome.

Writing: Look for an artwork that touches on a universal truth and, by describing the work, translate that truth into words. Select only those details that are pertinent. Edward Hopper or Jacob Lawrence would suit this assignment well, or you might want to concentrate on photography. For a wide range of photographers, see www.masters-of-photography.com or an identically titled website without the hyphens.

Page 49: Visiting my mother several years ago, I came upon the silver "muffinière"—an elaborate tower-shaped sugar-shaker—that had once stood between my father and me. (See photo at www.antrimhousebooks.com/seminar.) It took me back sixty years to the home front during World War II, when my father would sit across from me at breakfast, invisible behind the morning news. There was nothing for me but the back of his paper (so many faces of young soldiers newly dead) and that silver sugar-shaker stationed between us. Like the madeleine dipped in Proust's tea, it brought back not just the memory of a particular occasion but all the rest of my troubled sonship.

Writing: Let a household object (artful or not) lead to a meditation on the past.

Page 51: Another of my most indelible childhood memories is of my father carrying a terra cotta nude (see www.antrimhousebooks.com/seminar) from our rose garden to a basement room every fall. I was shocked that he embraced her (who looked suspiciously like my mother) in so unfatherly a fashion. What amazes me now is how easily he carried the heavy sculpture. I am not sure how conscious I was of the poem's mythical element when I was writing it (e.g., in Hades, many-headed Cerberus always keeps one eye open). Myths lurk so deep in our psyches that they often emerge spontaneously.

Writing: Art has traditionally provided the young with their first experience of forbidden fruit, be that art in *The National Geographic*, a stolen *Playboy*, a restroom or a lineup of Graeco-Roman statuary at the Metropolitan. Write about your own initiation through the medium of art.

Page 52: A definition of *art* is hard to come by. Would not a lineup of Zippo lighters qualify, especially if placed on a chest of antique keys like a sort of dentil molding?

Writing: Don't overlook *things* in your survey of art objects. To fully appreciate their poetic potential, have a look at Pablo Neruda's *Elementary Odes:* "Ode to Salt," "Ode to a Large Tuna in the Market," and others.* Naomi Shihab Nye* is another thingy poet. Their work may inspire a "thing poem" of your own.

Page 53 : Because my grandfather was a small man, his walking stick fit my mother perfectly. Its ornateness made it all the more fitting. It was good for more than Parkinson's.

Writing: Try a piece concerning the attachment of someone (perhaps a child or older person) to a possession, one whose history animates it or one that has for some other reason become indispensable.

Page 54: Certain names and events, though true, may be too improbably perfect to have any literary value. So it may be that I should have used a street name other than N. Carefree. Given my attachment to real toads, however, I kept it. On a map of Colorado Springs, you'll see that N. Carefree crosses Picturesque.

Writing: Try a poem in which a child reacts to fear, loneliness, deprivation or some other difficulty by turning to art. Consider writing wholly or partly in the child's voice.

Page 55: This is another poem resulting from a reading binge. The more I learned about Toulouse-Lautrec, the more I marveled at the complexity of his character. In the poem, I have used his six names to fashion a sort of literary trellis. As ever, structure supported the writing process, as has generally been the case for me, although I wouldn't go as far as Robert Frost, who quipped that writing free verse is like playing tennis without a net. All of which brings up interesting issues for further thought.

Writing: In Hermann Hesse's *Steppenwolf,* the protagonist discovers he is not a two-headed schizophrenic, as he feared, but thousands of different people in one being. Write a poem in which you describe the complex or multiple personality of any artist who particularly intrigues you. Define "artist" broadly enough to include personal acquaintances as well as "known artists." One possibility would be starting each section with "No" or some indication that the full truth has not been told.

Page 57: Nothing in Whistler's life is more fascinating and troubling than his creation of the outlandish Peacock Room as a setting for his painting "The Princess from the Land of Porcelain." The more I read about the Peacock Room, the stranger it seemed that he perpetrated such an outrage on an unsuspecting patron during the same period when he was creating some of his most lyrical and sensitive Nocturnes. I set out to write a poem that would partially exonerate him because of his second self, but the satirical glare was too much. When I made a last-ditch effort to save Whistler's reputation in the final stanza, it turned on me at the very end. A poem will do what a poem will do and there's no doing anything about it.

Source: The Peacock Room, created in London at the home of Frederick Leyland by James McNeill Whistler from 1876 to 1877, recreated at the Freer Gallery of the Smithsonian. For a virtual tour, visit www.asia.si.edu (exhibitions/on-lineexhibitions/ Peacock Room).

Writing: Refer to the previous assignment, but this time consider the possibility of a) describing the complex character of an artist through the words of several speakers as in the present poem; or b) letting the multiple sides of the artist all have their say. For more on what be called *literary cubism,* see p. 100.

Page 60: It was in a sidelong glance through a gallery window that I glimpsed the unknown painting on which "Self-Portrait at 14" is based. This may have led to the poem's interest in the mysterious world beyond glass that reflects the young artist and also allows her to see through it.

Something in us is both fascinated by and distrustful of mirrors (we sometimes cover them after a death). Writers have often depicted what lurks in them or what lies beyond (e.g., *Through the*

Looking Glass). Artists share this fascination with mirrors. Consider Wyeth's "The Revenant," in which the white-clad artist looks at his ghostly image in the mirror of a deserted house. The painting (at the New Britain Museum of American Art) is behind glass; thus, in certain lights the viewer sees not only him or herself superimposed on the painting but also other viewers. I am not sure what all this reflecting *means,* but it is interesting.

Writing: a) Reflect on reflections. Maybe if you explore "The Revenant" in a poem, its meaning will come clear. b) Taking a cue from "Self-Portrait at 14," write about someone looking through a darkened window (in a train, a car, a parlor) and seeing a self-portrait superimposed on a moving or unmoving background. c) Explore the possibilities of receding mirror images in double mirrors—as in the Hall of Mirrors at Versailles. See Hayden Carruth's "I,I,I" in *Scrambled Eggs & Whiskey.*

Page 61: The baroque clock of this poem is a composite of several different creations seen in museums and catalogues.

Writing: Compose a poem featuring one or more artifacts from an earlier period. There may be room for criticism of the degenerate times in which we live. For a lively example of an "artifact poem," see James Dickey's "Cherrylog Road," * which depicts a rendezvous in an automobile junkyard.

Page 62: Whittling is a good metaphor for the unpredictability of a poem. In preparing this book, that thought along with some suprising changes in my own life led me to revisit and revise the ending of "Whittler." Which brings up an interesting question. Is a poem necessarily dated, or can it be allowed to grow with its creator, assuming that by growing it comes closer to an essential truth that has been lying low in it?

Writing: a) Imagine yourself into the being of an artist or craftsman at work on a project. You might write your poem wholly or partially in the artist/craftsman's voice. You might also observe the artist-at-work from another's point of view—an artist's wife contemplating her husband's absorption in his work or a model watching the artist who paints or carves him/her (e.g., Victorine Meurend,* who posed for Manet's scandalous painting "Olympia" and many of his other works). Internet research may give you leads. b) Speculate on the nature of an unseen artwork or artist on the basis of whatever has been left behind—a costume or accessories, painting equipment, breakage, etc.

Page 64: This poem arose from a demonstration of kachina carving in Santa Fé. The carver was, like the kachinas themselves, charming, witty, irreverent, and reverent. The Mount referred to is Mt. Taylor, traditional home of the kachina gods.

Writing: Describe the creation of a religious work (Michelangelo on his scaffold painting the Sistine Chapel, for instance). Try to depict the realities as well as the sublimities of such creation.

Page 65: I have always been fascinated by Hopi and Zuni ritual and mythology, especially as displayed in kachina ceremonies. Like other "primitive" rituals, these are works of art. In them the kachina gods are played by gorgeously costumed human kachinas, who take on divine attributes. See the Antrim House website for kachina dolls representing the principals in "Solstice."

Writing: Peruse works such as Frank Waters' *Masked Gods* (Hopi and Navajo ritual) and Joseph Campbell's *The Hero with a Thousand Faces* (world-wide ritual and mythology). Poetry is sure to come of such reading.

Page 66: Stanley Kunitz says the poet should raise his or her life to the level of legend. I am not sure I want to wear a red *L* on my chest, but I do think life becomes more interesting when we see ourselves as characters in a film or novel and realize that experiences which at first appear prosaic can in fact be legendary. My trek into a remote section of Utah's Canyonlands some years ago seemed ordinary enough, compared to the prehistoric pictographs I encountered there (see the front cover for one example). But when I began to write about that trek, I came to see it in a new light. My voice became someone else's, maybe Kokopelli's.

Writing: a) In a photograph album, look for mementos of a journey, especially one that took strange turns, involved unexpected dangers, or revealed mysteries (e.g., a childhood excursion on Halloween night or a return to the family homestead). Translate your memory into a poem. Remember that the act of writing will free the mythologist in you. b) Write a poem inspired by a primitive artifact, work of art, or site—anything from an Irish circle fort to the Black Virgin of Guadalupe.

Page 68: Inspired by the photo of a site I'd visited (see the Antrim House website), this poem began as a sort of travelogue. Revision was helpful. In addition to removing verbiage, I tried to add metaphorical muscle, as in "raising their lost lives by the power of Owl and Coyote and Crow." I also tried to sharpen the poem's focus on the theme of transformation; among other changes was the addition of a reference to the "lost lives" of the Navajo boys.

Writing: Look through photographs of places you have visited. When you have finished a first draft based on one of them, revisit the draft to see if your poem is sharply focused on a "universal concept." If not, sharpen its focus. Also check to see if it contains verbiage or unnecessary explanations. Are its images (from all five senses) memorable, or are they obscured by words? Is its language pretentious? Could it ride more squarely on simple nouns and verbs? Remember, revision is not dickering: it is reseeing.

Page 69: Don't overlook buildings as works of art. Yeats' tower, whose restoration was completed in 1919 and in which he and his family lived in for several summers, is as much an artistic creation as any of his poems. For me, however, it was at first a disappointment, then something of a terror, but in the end a separate peace short-lived and therefore much to be treasured.

Writing: Consider some of your own moments of truth arising from buildings, rooms, or artistically conceived places (gardens and bridges, for instance), and write about one of them. Don't be afraid of risking the sort of "absurdity" Lawrence Ferlinghetti recommends to an acrobatic poet; in particular, risk the romanticism found in Raymond Carver's "tenderly tough" poems.* We all know the grime of life, and it's fairly easy to write about. Its opposite we see less often, and it's terribly hard to write about effectively, therefore all the more important.

Page 71: If you are not well-versed in Sappho's work and life, a google-crawl will be interesting and may throw light on the poem.

Writing: Try a poem in the voice of someone infatuated by, ambivalent about, or furious at an artist, defining "artist" broadly (a teacher as seen by a student, Henri Matisse as seen by Amélie Matisse, W. B. Yeats as seen by Maude Gonne).

Page 72: It is now clear that Napoleon Bonaparte was poisoned by arsenic applied to his wine at dinner. The poison caused bloating, a slow death, and miraculous preservation of his remains. At least one biographer thinks Napoleon suspected he was being poisoned and was too depressed to take action.

Writing: Describe the way someone turns to art, broadly defined, to fend off despair. One thinks of prisoners scratching designs on their cell walls. In fact, what prisoners have accomplished behind bars is impressive. Without prisons neither *Pilgrim's Progress* nor *Don Quixote* would exist. Consider the many kinds of despair that have led to creation, from unhappy family situations to disease, depression, and other sorts of imprisonment.

Page 74: The characters in this poem are real, but the main event is imagined. There are several works of art in the poem, including that marvelous Archimboldo portrait of Rudolf II as Veretumnus, whose features are composed entirely of fruits and vegetables (see www.topofart.com). What intrigues me about the Emperor is the fact that in addition to being one of the world's greatest patrons of art, he was an entirely self-centered ignoramus. Tycho Brahe was also one of the world's greats, a ground-breaking (even though inaccurate) astronomer, as well as an egomaniac richly deserving his burst bladder. I am amused by the way Brahe and the Emperor trump one another subtly enough that they manage to stave off an interpersonal religious war on the eve of the Thirty Years War. I am less amused by the sort of arrogance both principals display: on a national scale, it would soon plunge much of the Seventeenth Century world into a conflict more terrible than any preceding it. "Under the Sun" turned out to be less lighthearted than I'd expected.

Writing: Beginning with a photograph, sculpture or painting (anything from a photo-op picture of some contemporary political figure to "Bonaparte Crossing the Alps" by Louis David*), debunk a self-important world leader, contemporary, historical or legendary. Remember that the wit is mightier than the whip. Laughter is the ultimate answer to despotism, the sort of laughter that has a dagger up its sleeve. Feel free to create a totally imaginary event featuring your debunkee.

Page 76: Babylon, a center of the arts, was itself a work of art and has inspired many artists. One thinks of William Blake's glorious rendition of Nebuchadnezzar,* the Babylonian king and scourge of the Jews, who was sentenced by Jehovah to crawl the face of the Earth like a wild beast, part ox, part bird of prey. In the Bible there are several Babylons, which the poem has folded into a single doomed metropolis. One is the site of the Tower of Babel in "Genesis"; another is the semi-legendary Babylon of the Hanging Gardens; and a third is the city of the Babylonian Captivity, where Daniel was thrown to the lions and later became the prophet who read handwriting on the palace wall. The ruins of historical Babylon exist in present-day Iraq, next to Saddam Hussein's erstwhile presidential palace.*

Every poet should read at least the following books of the Bible: "Genesis," "Exodus," "Kings" (I and II), "Samuel" (I and II),

"Ecclesiastes," "Esther," "Job," "Ruth," "Song of Solomon," "Daniel," the four Gospels, "Corinthians" (I and II), and "Revelation." Be sure that you choose the King James version of the Bible. There is more to a Mary *great with child* than to one who is *pregnant*. The King James Bible is one of the great works of literary art.

Writing: When you come up from the Bible for air, you'll need no assignment. You'll create your own.

Page 78: This is another poem that benefited from research (into the married life of the Hoppers). But it is also as confessional a poem as I have written. I hope it is sufficiently universal to justify itself.

An on-line search will lead to many of the Hoppers mentioned. For "Two Comedians" see www.soho-art.com.

Writing: Think back to a time when you (perhaps as a child) were amazed, frightened, or appalled by what you saw in a museum (of natural history, dolls, witchcraft, native culture, etc.). Write about that experience. If you focus on a museum visit made as an adult (e.g., to a Holocaust museum), don't overlook the possibility that your memory may lead in a confessional direction. Bear in mind that confessional poems are risky, since all too often they are more personal than pertinent. However, if they describe behavior we all relate to, they can serve an important purpose. If your poem deviates from the museum visit that inspired it, be of good cheer. One of the purposes of this book is to suggest that a well-conceived "art poem" is always less about art than about life—the life of the poet, the life of everyone.

Page 80: Christmas has inspired many kinds of art, such as the Advent calendar with all those little doors or windows to open, one for each day of December until Christmas, when the last opening shows the manger. Advent calendars call to mind the search of the Magi and perhaps, as I discovered in writing this poem, other searches as well. The dark that crept into "Advent

Calendar" took me by surprise.

Writing: a) In the same way that "A Ring Around the Rosy" had its origins in the days of the Bubonic Plague, when a burgher might breathe through a nosegay (a pocketful of posies) to avoid becoming a "rosie," so too can apparently innocuous objects be related to dire situations. Let such an object lead you to a poem depicting some sadness or even what Mr. Kurtz calls "the horror, the horror." b) Like Edvard Munch in "The Scream" or Allen Ginsberg in "Howl" and "Kaddish," give vent to a darkness in yourself—a grief, a despair, a terror. Let a news photo or painting be the catalyst for your howl. Don't hold back.

Page 81: The source of this poem is an untitled work (crayon on paper) by my grandson, who had not quite turned three at the time of creation (see www.antrimhousebooks.com/seminar.) It is hard to guess what was in his mind, perhaps joy in the violence of the scene. Presumably, the artist was unaware of the Flight into Egypt, by which the Holy Family escaped the wrath of Herod, but his crayoning seems to know about it, which gives the narrator an opening.

Writing: Compose a poem based on the artwork of a child. Decide whether you want to write from the child's point of view or an older narrator's. An alternative would be to write a two-part poem from dual points of view. Don't be afraid of mixing emotions and moods. Why should the serious not cohabit with the comic, as it does in writers as various as Billy Collins and William Shakespeare?

Page 82: Try writing a poem in which something looks like or poses like a work of art, or in which art comes to life.

Page 83: An exhibit of carousel horses in Hartford's Wadsworth Atheneum was so exotic that I suspended all disbelief. And where better to do so than in the city of Wallace Stevens, for whom Imagination was godly? To see examples of the horses, which now ride the carousel in Hartford, search *Bushnell Park Carousel* on the internet.

Writing: Visit an art museum or conjure up a museum visit and report on the behavior of observers and/or preservers of art. You might include art objects themselves as characters. Let your imagination romp. If a dowager wants to stage a heist, so be it.

Page 84: Whenever we dress up, down, or across, we become art objects—anything from a Zuni kachina dancer to a child decked out in her mother's gewgaws.

For a famous Seventeenth Century clothes poem, see Robert Herrick's "On Julia's Clothes."* More contemporary treatments are Billy Collins' "Victoria's Secret"* and Mark Doty's "Couture" (in *Atlantis*). Erica Jong's "In Praise of Clothes"* and Billy Collins' "Taking off Emily Dickinson's Clothes"* have much to say about the joy of undressing.

Writing: a) Compose a poem focused on adult "dress-up": a lover's, a lady of the night's, a cross-dresser's. b) Describe the art of un-dressing (yourself or someone else). c) Describe a child's art-in-motion—the parading of a fabulous costume, an unwatched dance, a spontaneous song. If the child expresses fury, frustration, or animal joy, so much the better.

Page 85: Based on a photo of my mother as a schoolgirl skating in clown costume (see Antrim House website/seminar page), this poem might lead you to an art-based poem focused on an older person looking to childhood (or a child) for solace or inspiration.

Page 86: Make an archaeological find (e.g., Schliemann's unearthing of Troy*) a metaphor for some sort of personal discovery.

Page 87: Thoreau said a writer should delve for words whose roots still cling to them. Here, the phrase "fabulous thing" is meant in its root sense. If you are unfamiliar with the fable of the phoenix bird, do some research on the web or in a mythology handbook.

Writing: In some ways, a work-in-progress such as the one in this poem is more interesting than the final product, as is evident in one of the best descriptions of artistic process, Tracy Chevalier's novel *Girl with a Pearl Earring*. Describe a process of artistic creation that has a strong emotional quotient (e.g., a child in the midst of making a first valentine, a sculptor carving a memorial for a deceased love, a divorcée constructing a voodoo doll of her ex). Consider the artist's private life when composing your piece. And write from experience, remembering that discoveries made during research or conversation are part of your experience.

Page 88: Once again the poem led the poet—this time to the open waters of biblical legend. If you are unfamiliar with the story of Jacob's Ladder, refer to the concordance in a Bible or web-search *Jacob's Ladder, Bible*.

Writing: a) Various forms of "love-art" are traditional, from belly-dancing to high school rock art and other kinds of graffiti. Focus a poem on one example. b) Taking your cue from any work of art in which love is central, from the lustiest to the most sublime, try a love poem, perhaps the easiest sort of poem to write badly and the hardest to write well. You might want to make this a "persona poem," adopting the voice of someone in the artwork you have chosen. You might also want to emulate Plato (whose *Symposium* is a well-wrought ladder leading from lower to higher forms of love) by incorporating more than one rung of love in your poem. In looking for apt art, consider Fragonard, Chagall, Klimt, Renoir, Caravaggio, and Vermeer, as well as photographers such as Robert Mapplethorpe (all represented on-line). Enjoy the journey on which your writing takes you.

Photo by Pit Pinegar

Rennie McQuilkin's poetry has appeared in publications such as *The Atlantic, The Southern Review, The Yale Review, The Hudson Review, Poetry,* and *The American Scholar.* He is the author of nine poetry collections, two of which have won awards; and his *Selected Poems* will be released in 2007. McQuilkin has received fellowships from the National Endowment for the Arts as well as the Connecticut Commission on the Arts, and for many years he directed the Sunken Garden Poetry Festival, which he co-founded at Hill-Stead Museum in Farmington, CT. In 2003 he received a Lifetime Achievement Award from the Connecticut Center for the Book.

To order *Private Collection* or other Antrim House titles see www.antrimhousebooks.com or contact the publisher at 860-217-0023, P.O. Box 111, Tariffville, CT 06081.